as a

# Gladiator

*An Interactive History Adventure*

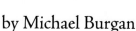

by Michael Burgan

Consultant:
Kelly Olson, PhD
Associate Professor and Graduate Chair
Dept. of Classical Studies and Faculty of Law
The University of Western Ontario
London, Ontario

Raintree is an imprint of Capstone Global Library Limited, a company incorporated in England and Wales having its registered office at 7 Pilgrim Street, London, EC4V 6LB – Registered company number: 6695582

www.raintreepublishers.co.uk
myorders@raintreepublishers.co.uk

Text © Capstone Global Library Limited 2015
The moral rights of the proprietor have been asserted.

ISBN 978 1 474 70677 3
19 18 17 16 15
10 9 8 7 6 5 4 3 2 1

Printed and bound in China

British Library Cataloguing in Publication Data
A full catalogue record for this book is available from the British Library.

Photo Credits
akg-images: Peter Connolly, 52; Alamy: North Wind Picture Archives, 74; The Art Archive: NGS Image Collection/H.M. Herget, 12; The Bridgeman Art Library: ©Look and Learn/Private Collection, 32, ©Look and Learn/Private Collection/Angus McBride, 18, 25, ©Look and Learn/Private Collection/Roger Payne, 69, ©Look and Learn/Private Collection/Patrick Nicolle, 97; Corbis: Christie's Images, 60, 79; Getty Images Inc.: The Bridgeman Art Library/Edmund Blair Leighton, 95, Fedor Andreevich Bronnikov, 39, Private Collection/Harry Green, 40, Time Life Pictures/Mansell, 91; The Granger Collection, New York, 100; Johnny Shumate, cover, 6, 70; North Wind Picture Archives, 37; Shutterstock: LoopAll, cover background, Sandra van der Steen, 102; Super Stock Inc.: Fine Art Photographic Library, 86; Reproduced from *YoungReading: Gladiators* by permission of Usborne Publishing, 83–85 Saffron Hill, London EC1N 8RT, UK. Copyright © 2010 Usborne Publishing Ltd', 29, 47, 58

# TABLE OF CONTENTS

# About your ADVENTURE

YOU are living in Italy during the time of the Roman Empire. People who settled on a series of hills near the River Tiber built the city of Rome. Over time it grew and became powerful.

You and your fellow gladiators fight in events called games. Perhaps you'll earn prize money and fame. But if you lose, you could face painful wounds or an early death.

Chapter one sets the scene. Then you choose which path to read. Follow the directions at the bottom of each page. The choices you make will change your outcome. After you finish one path, go back and read the others for more adventures and facts about life as a gladiator.

*YOU CHOOSE the path*
*you take through history.*

Gladiators called thraeces fought with a curved sword called a sica.

# Gladiators and the glory of Rome

A walk through Rome around 100 BC showed a wealthy, bustling city of about 1 million people. Residents strolled along stone streets as wagons and carts rushed by. The poor lived in crowded wooden buildings, while rich citizens built grand homes.

Rome's greatness came through war. Its soldiers conquered lands across Europe, North Africa, and Asia. The victories gave Rome new sources of food and tribute in gold and other precious materials.

*Turn the page.*

Slavery was common in all ancient societies around the Mediterranean Sea. Roman slaves were often foreign soldiers and civilians captured after a battle. Some were criminals. A few were children abandoned at birth. Wherever they came from, most slaves faced a hard life working on farms, in mines, or at small factories. Slaves also served as most of the gladiators who fought during the *ludi*, the public games.

Gladiator matches developed out of private funeral ceremonies for important Romans. Rome's first recorded gladiator match took place in 264 BC at the funeral of Junius Brutus Pera in the city's Forum Boarium.

By 100 BC gladiators were the central part of games held to entertain the people of Rome. A wealthy or politically powerful Roman, called an *editor*, sponsored the games.

Dozens of pairs of gladiators might battle during the four- to five-day games. The events also included chariot races and athletic contests. Wild animal hunts took place in the same amphitheatre where the gladiators fought. Sometimes criminals were also executed before the crowds.

Not all gladiators were slaves. Some were criminals. A few were free citizens who chose careers as gladiators. A few women also entered the arena. Most of them were slaves or prisoners. Whatever their background, gladiators trained hard at special schools. Gladiators became experts at using a particular kind of weapon. Those known as *murmillones* used a sword called a *gladius*, which was the source of the gladiators' name. Other types of gladiators included the *thraex, retiarius, hoplomachus*, and *secutor*.

*Turn the page.*

Since most were slaves and prisoners, gladiators were not considered respected members of society. But once in the arena, their skills and willingness to face death impressed many Romans.

The games weren't always a fight to the death. The first Roman emperor, Augustus, ruled from 27 BC to AD 14. He stopped the tradition of gladiator matches ending in the death of one fighter. But later emperors did allow such deadly fights. And if a gladiator didn't die in combat, he might be killed after losing a fight. However, a crowd favourite might have his life spared. Still, life as a gladiator was dangerous, and few lived to an old age.

ITALY, AD 79

*ITALY*

*Adriatic Sea*

APENNINE MOUNTAINS

Rome ○

∧ *Mount Garganus*

**Capua**
**Naples** ○ ∧ *Mount Vesuvius*
○ **Pompeii**

○ **Thurii**

*Mediterranean Sea*

○ City
⋀⋀ MOUNTAIN RANGE

| 0 | 150 mi. |
| 0 | 150 km |

*SICILY*

*Strait of Messina*

Choose the gladiator's adventure you want to explore:

✠To take part in the rebellion led by the gladiator
Spartacus in 73 BC, turn to page **13**.

✠To be a free citizen training as a gladiator in
Pompeii in AD 79, turn to page **41**.

✠To be a veteran gladiator at the Roman
amphitheatre in AD 107, turn to page **71**.

Most Roman gladiators were men who were either captured or born into slavery.

# CHAPTER 2

# Spartacus' rebellion

You walk down the dusty streets of the Roman city of Capua, heavy metal chains dragging from your legs. On all sides of you, other chained men plod along. As the hot sun beats down, a stick prods your shoulder.

"You there, slave!" a man calls out. "What's your name?"

You look up and see the *lanista* Lentulus Vatia, your new owner.

You tell Vatia your name as sweat pours down your face.

*Turn the page.*

"Ah, a Celt," Vatia says. "You must be a good fighter. You Celts are so fearless. But I can't have my gladiators fighting with foreign names. I'm going to call you Felix. You know what that means?"

You nod. Felix is Latin for "lucky." You wonder how lucky you will be.

Soon you pass Capua's amphitheatre. There you and your fellow gladiators will entertain the crowds. The school is nearby.

At the school several hundred slaves live and work together, training to become gladiators. One of Vatia's workers takes off your chains and throws you into a tiny room. Inside, another gladiator lies on a bed stuffed with reeds.

"How did you become a slave?" he asks.

"My mother was captured years ago, before I was born. She was made a slave, and I was born one."

"You know how to fight?" your roommate asks.

"A bit." You see scars on the man's body, from past contests in the arena. "Not like you, I'm sure."

"Maybe it would be better if you never see the inside of the arena. You might not live."

"There's nothing I can do," you say. "I'm a slave."

Your roommate leans closer. His voice is now a whisper. "We're tired of how Vatia treats us. We're rebelling. The murmillo Spartacus and some others have it all planned. Will you join us?"

✢ To join the rebellion, turn to page 16.

✢ To refuse, turn to page 23.

"I would rather die fighting for my freedom than live like this," you say.

"I agree," your roommate responds. He offers a beefy hand. "My name is Acamas."

"So what should I do?" you ask.

"Just wait for my signal after dinner. I'll show you where to go."

As several hours pass, your stomach begins to tighten. You shouldn't have lied when you told Acamas you could fight. You've never held a sword before. But you're strong, and you want to help the rebels.

After dinner you and the other gladiators start walking to your rooms. Acamas tells you to go back to the kitchen. The kitchen has knives and iron rods called spits used for cooking meat. You can use them as weapons.

The two of you stop, turn, and run towards the kitchen. You suppose that 200 other gladiators are now rushing towards the building. But the guards are waiting for them!

"Someone must have told them," Acamas says. "Come on, keep running."

"But they have swords," you say. "We have nothing to fight with."

"They have swords, but we outnumber them. This is for your freedom!"

You stop and look at the waiting guards.

"Do what you want," Acamas says as he sprints on. "But I'm going."

✝To keep running, turn to page **18**.

✝To turn back, turn to page **26**.

You run after Acamas and the others, heading for the kitchen. Ahead of you, the other gladiators have rushed past the guards. You try not to look at the bleeding bodies of the men stabbed by the guards. Some of the Roman guards lie dead too. Gladiators turned the soldiers' own swords against them.

Famed gladiator Spartacus (centre, front) led a huge slave rebellion in Capua.

You enter the kitchen, which is still smoky from the cooking of the evening meal. "Take all the tools you can," a muscular gladiator orders. His eyes are sharp, and the other men quickly obey him. You look at Acamas, who says just one word: "Spartacus".

You grab a spit. With enough force, you can easily shove it through a guard's neck.

"Hurry!" Spartacus shouts, as gladiators and guards continue to fight outside the kitchen. You take a knife and follow Acamas and the others through the kitchen's back door. You are now part of a force of about 75 gladiators.

Outside the school, you spot a wagon on the road ahead. "We're in luck," Acamas says. "Vatia had just sent that wagon to some gladiatorial games outside Capua. It's loaded with weapons."

*Turn the page.*

Spartacus orders a small group of gladiators to run ahead and stop the wagon. You help tie up the Romans riding in the wagon while Acamas and others unload the weapons. Spartacus then gathers the gladiators together.

"The Romans will send soldiers to track us down like animals," Spartacus says. "If the troops catch us, we'll be killed." Spartacus walks among the men. He stops in front of you.

"You're one of the new ones?" he asks. You nod.

"Are you ready to fight? Ready to die? If not, leave us now."

✜To stay with the rebels, go to page **21**.
✜To leave the rebels, turn to page **28**.

You look Spartacus in the eye. "I want to go with you."

"Then let's go!" Spartacus yells, motioning to you and the others to follow.

In the following days, Spartacus leads you to Vesuvius, a volcano about 32 kilometres (20 miles) south of Capua. You help to build a camp in the woods on the mountainside. Some days you join a group that steals food from nearby farms. Other times you raid the homes of rich landowners, taking their gold, silver, and other valuables. Spartacus always divides the goods equally among the men.

As the weeks pass, slaves from the countryside join the group. So do a few poor free Romans. A small police force from Capua tries to end the rebellion. Spartacus leads you to defeat the police in a short battle.

*Turn the page.*

Soon word reaches the camp that the Romans are sending a larger force after you. About 3,000 Roman soldiers set up a camp below yours on the mountain. Spartacus orders a surprise attack.

At Spartacus' signal, you storm the camp. The Romans run in every direction. You follow Oenomaus, a Celtic commander under Spartacus.

Oenomaus swings his sword at a soldier. The Roman returns the thrust with his weapon. Just then a javelin whistles through the air. It strikes Oenomaus, sending him to his knees.

✢ "Oenomaus!" you cry, rushing over to help him.

✢ "Go back!" the commander shouts. "I'm done for. Join the others."

✢To join the other rebels, turn to page 24.

✢To help Oenomaus, turn to page 29.

You're not about to risk your life for a rebellion led by a man you've never even met. "No thanks," you tell your roommate, whose name is Acamas.

He shrugs. "Well, it's your loss."

Acamas says the gladiators will rebel when they leave their rooms for dinner. When the dinner call comes, you stay behind. But after a few minutes, you get curious. You leave your room and slowly walk out into the hall. You see Acamas among a large group of gladiators, ready to charge. Maybe you should join them after all.

✠

✠

*Turn to page* **26.**

Before you can move, the Roman stabs Oenomaus. He falls to the ground, dead. You say a prayer to the gods for him and then rush forward into the Roman camp. Few Romans are eager to fight. They flee, leaving behind their dead and wounded. You grab their weapons and food.

Spartacus' army grows until it reaches at least 40,000 men. For a time the army camps in the city of Thurii. You now have enough experience to train the new members of the army. Some men make simple shields out of woven branches. Others melt down their old slave chains to make swords.

As time goes on, Spartacus and the Celtic commander Crixus decide to split the army. Crixus will head east, towards the Adriatic Sea. Spartacus will head north. Your friend Acamas looks at you.

Spartacus' rebel army soon became skilled in fighting with tridents and swords.

"I'm going with Crixus," he says. "What will you do?"

✠To go with Crixus, turn to page **31**.

✠To go with Spartacus, turn to page **34**.

You decide you're no rebel. You stand there as your roommate and the other gladiators rush forward. In a few seconds, the first of them reach the guards. The guards thrust their swords left and right. Gladiators scream as they fall to the ground. You know you've made the right decision.

You turn back to go to your room. Out of the darkness steps a guard, his sword drawn. "Where are you going, slave?" the guard demands.

"Just back to my room," you stammer. "I was late leaving for dinner, then I saw the other gladiators running towards me. I had heard there was a rebellion, but I wanted no part of it."

The guard steps forward. He puts the tip of his sword to your chest.

"You're one of the new ones, aren't you?" the guard asks. You nod.

"You're no different from the others. All you filthy slaves are liars."

"No!" you cry, dropping to one knee. "Please, I'm no rebel!"

You grab the guard's leg, begging for your life. But with a quick thrust, the blade of his sword slices into your chest. You die, never having entered the arena.

**THE END**

*To follow another path, turn to page 11.*
*To read the conclusion, turn to page 101.*

"I'm no fighter," you say. "I wanted freedom, but now I'm not sure."

Some of the men begin to hoot and shout insults. Spartacus quietens them with a wave of his hand. "Better to tell the truth now than get in our way when the fighting starts. Go."

Spartacus then turns to the other gladiators. "The rest of you – follow me!"

"Goodbye," Acamas calls to you. "I hope you can keep your freedom."

"Me too," you say softly. You head away from Capua, knowing troops will soon be after Spartacus and the others. You cut across a field, not sure where you will go. But for now, you are free.

## THE END

*To follow another path, turn to page 11.*
*To read the conclusion, turn to page 101.*

You can't let a fellow Celt die like this. With a scream, you charge at the Roman. He stops his thrust at Oenomaus to look at you. Sweat drips from under his iron helmet, and blood trickles down his arm. One of Oenomaus' blows must have nicked him. As you reach him, the Roman steps aside, and you run past him. The other gladiators have been training you, but you are still clumsy with a sword. You get ready to charge again.

Spartacus' army and the Roman soldiers fought many bloody battles.

*Turn the page.*

"Watch out!" Oenomaus calls weakly to you. Oenomaus is near death, but from his position, he sees what you can't. As you turn, another Roman jumps towards you. In his right hand is a dagger. You try to step aside, but the blade catches you just above your armour. A sharp pain cuts through your shoulder.

Together you and the Roman fall to the ground. You reach to grab his arm as he prepares to stab again. But the Roman is stronger. The blade pierces your neck, killing you instantly.

✛

## THE END

*To follow another path, turn to page 11.*
*To read the conclusion, turn to page 101.*

Crixus leads you to the area around Mount Garganus. The land is covered with oak forests, giving you plenty of places to hide. But the Romans soon track you down. A Roman army with as many men as yours prepares to attack.

As the battle begins, you raise your sword and run to the nearest Roman. You find a weak spot in the soldier's armour. With one thrust of your sword, you kill the Roman soldier and run towards another.

The fighting drags on for several hours. A Roman sword catches your arm, but the blade barely scratches you. You keep fighting as the bodies of your dead friends pile up around you.

Acamas calls to you. He has moved towards the back of the fighting. "We don't stand a chance. We should run."

*Turn the page.*

Many of your friends are dead. So is Crixus. This is no time to be a hero. You and Acamas run for the woods nearby. The Romans chase you for a short distance, but they know they have won the battle. They soon turn back.

Spartacus vowed not to give up his fight against the Romans.

You and Acamas stop in the woods. "Our army is done for," Acamas says.

"But Spartacus is still fighting," you reply.

"We don't know that. Maybe the Romans got him too. It's only a question of time."

"Let's go back to Thurii," you say. "The rebels are still in control there. We can live safely there – for now."

Acamas agrees. It will be a long trip to Thurii. But you have your best friend with you, and you are free.

## THE END

*To follow another path, turn to page 11.*
*To read the conclusion, turn to page 101.*

You walk over and shake Acamas' hand.

"Good luck, friend," you say. "But I am staying with Spartacus."

As Crixus' army leaves, Spartacus prepares to march too. You head to the Apennine Mountains, but the Romans soon find you there. Spartacus' army now includes cavalry and is three times the size of the Roman force. You quickly defeat the Romans.

One day a messenger from Crixus' army arrives. "I have bad news," he says. "The Romans defeated us in our last battle. Worst of all, Crixus was killed."

As the months go on, Spartacus defeats every army sent after his forces. But Rome keeps sending better troops and generals. In the autumn of 72 BC, word reaches the camp that the important general Crassus now leads the Romans.

You are camped with Spartacus when a messenger brings more bad news. Crassus and his men have killed about 6,000 of Spartacus' soldiers at another camp. Soon they will come for Spartacus.

"We need to get some distance between our army and Crassus," Spartacus tells you. "We'll march to the coast and cross the Strait of Messina to the island of Sicily."

When you reach the coast, Spartacus makes a deal with pirates to take an advance party of 2,000 rebels across the narrow strait to Sicily. The small, fast pirate ships can't hold your entire army. Spartacus pays the pirates the money they demand. But instead of taking you to Sicily, they sail away.

*Turn the page.*

You expect Spartacus to be angry. Instead, he shrugs. "If the pirates won't take us, we'll get across ourselves." He orders you and the other men to build rafts. But when you launch the rafts, the strait's current is too strong to cross.

Soon after, another Roman attack kills thousands more of your fellow rebels. You follow Spartacus as he retreats towards the central part of southern Italy. Crassus' army isn't far away. Some of the rebels find the Romans digging trenches, preparing for battle. The rebel force attacks, and Spartacus orders all of you into battle.

The Roman soldiers throw their javelins, striking many of the rebels in the front lines. The Romans then charge forwards, their swords drawn. Spartacus marches towards Crassus. He manages to kill two Roman soldiers before a javelin soars through the air and pierces his leg.

In 71 BC, Roman soldiers killed Spartacus on the battlefield.

Spartacus falls to one knee, trying to block the Roman swords. But your wounded general can't hold off so many men. To your horror, Spartacus falls to the ground, dead.

*Turn the page.*

With their leader gone, your fellow rebels lose their courage. You join many of them as they run from the battlefield. Thousands more rebels lie dead.

You and other rebels head for the nearby mountains. Crassus and his men are right behind you. Finally, exhausted, you fall, and the Romans capture you.

The soldiers order you to march. Several days later, you reach Capua. Along a main road you see a row of wooden crosses.

"They're going to crucify us!" you say to the others, horrified.

The Romans put you and the 6,000 other rebels on the crosses. You die slowly. Your dead body reminds other gladiators what will happen to them if they try to rebel.

The Romans crucified the rest of Spartacus' rebel army.

✚

## THE END

*To follow another path, turn to page 11.*
*To read the conclusion, turn to page 101.*

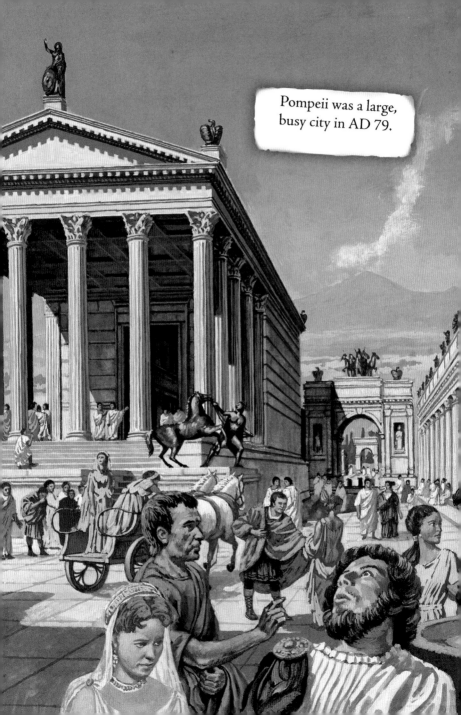

Pompeii was a large, busy city in AD 79.

# CHAPTER 3

# Gladiator in training

You're walking with your father to Pompeii's school for gladiators. Ahead, you see the great volcano Vesuvius. Hundreds of years ago, it erupted with fire and ash, but now it seems calm. No one fears another eruption.

But you are a little bit afraid of your father. You have never seen him so angry. He's upset that you want to become a gladiator.

"You know what this means?" he asks. "You'll lose all your rights as a Roman citizen. You'll be no more than a slave."

*Turn the page.*

"I understand, Father," you say. "But I am tired of being poor. We're not slaves, but we might as well be. I could earn lots of money if I fight well."

Your father stops. "Then go. But don't expect us to speak to you again. May the gods protect you."

As you walk, you pass the amphitheatre. As a young boy, you watched the gladiators fight there. You often wondered what it would be like to battle there yourself. Soon you reach the school. The lanista, Pomponius Faustinus, stands outside.

"So the young volunteer, the *auctoratus*, is ready to become a gladiator," Pomponius says.

"Yes, sir," you reply.

"Remember, you will be my slave for five years. But I will pay you for your victories – assuming you fight well enough to win."

You nod. "All right then," Pomponius says. "You know the oath?"

You have been practising the oath for days. All gladiators must swear it as they begin their training. You speak clearly, "I will endure to be burned, to be bound, to be beaten, and to be killed by the sword."

"Good," Pomponius says. "All that's left is for you to sign a contract – and choose how you will fight. Will you use a sword? Or would you rather fight with the trident and the net?"

✠To fight with a trident, turn to page 44.
✠To fight with a sword, turn to page 46.

Many gladiators use swords. But only the retiarius fights with a trident and a net. Pomponius likes your choice. He can always use a good net man.

The lanista leads you into the barracks. A man about 35 years old approaches you. You notice many scars on his body.

"I am Cresces," he says. "I'll be your trainer."

You follow Cresces to a corner of the courtyard where weapons are stored. Cresces hands you a trident and a dagger. "You'll use the dagger to kill your opponent, if necessary." Cresces pulls out the round net. It's about 3 metres (10 feet) wide. Lead weights along the edge make it easier to throw. "Use this to trap him first. Thrust your trident to hold off his sword. Then move in with the net. But you'll have months of training before you fight for real."

You watch the men across the courtyard, practising their skills. You study the scars on Cresces' body. If some had been just a little higher or lower, he wouldn't be alive to teach you. You ask yourself, "Do I really have the courage to be a gladiator?"

✠To continue as a gladiator, turn to page **49**.
✠To give up and leave the school, turn to page **55**.

You have often held your grandfather's sword, which he kept from his days as a soldier. But you don't want to fight with the short, straight sword that most gladiators use.

"I want to be a thraex and fight with a *sica*," you tell Pomponius.

"Good," he says. "The crowd always loves a talented thraex."

Pomponius takes you to meet Telephus, one of the instructors at the school. You have seen him fight many times. He's one of Pompeii's greatest gladiators.

Telephus pulls on the high leg guards most thraeces wear. Then he puts on his helmet and picks up a small, square shield. It's bent so it wraps around his hand. Finally he picks up a sica, the curved sword.

"I'll show you some basic moves," he says. "Then you'll begin to train on the poles."

All across the courtyard, you see novicii using wooden swords as they move around and thrust at poles stuck in the ground. But you want some real action.

Novice gladiators trained with dummies and wooden swords.

*Turn the page.*

"Telephus," you say. "I've seen many thraex fight in the amphitheatre. I've used a sword before. I don't want to wait. I want to fight for real, right now."

Telephus laughs. "So you're a brave one." He comes close to you, holding the sica up close to your face. "Or stupid. Do you know how many men I've killed in the arena? Even in practice, I could slice you before you knew what hit you. Are you sure you want to spar with me?"

✝To train with the other gladiators, turn to page **52**.

✝To spar with Telephus, turn to page **63**.

This is the life you chose. "When do we start training?" you ask.

"Good," Cresces says. "An eager novicius. Come on."

You walk across the courtyard, where wooden poles rise out of the ground. You see other young gladiators attacking the poles as if they were opponents. The novicii use wooden weapons and shields.

"That's how you'll start," Cresces explains. "And as you get better, you'll practise with real weapons."

In the weeks that follow, Cresces shows you how to hold your trident and net. As a retiarius, you wear almost no armour. You can move more quickly than your opponent. But you need that speed to avoid his sword.

*Turn the page.*

After practice you join the other gladiators in the dining hall. You stand next to Florus, your closest friend at the school. He is a secutor. Similar to a murmillo, he uses a gladius and large shield when he fights.

You each take a helping of bean and barley stew. You eat the same thing day after day. You learn that people sometimes call the gladiators "barley men."

"Why do we eat so much of this?" you ask Florus. "I'm sick of it."

"It makes you fat," he says. "And that's good."

"But won't I be slower if I'm fat?"

Florus pinches a roll of flab around his stomach. "The fat protects you. Makes it harder for your opponent to score a deadly wound."

Florus is a veteran gladiator. The veterans are divided into ranks, depending on the number of times they have won. The gladiators at the school are like a family. But you know that one day, you might have to kill a man you consider a friend.

It's the day of your first fight. Pomponius has set up the matches. "You will fight Florus," he tells you.

You gulp. You knew you would fight a secutor, since retiarii are always matched with them. But how can you fight your best friend?

✞To refuse to fight Florus, turn to page 57.
✞To fight him, turn to page 59.

Telephus gives you a wooden sword and a wicker shield. "These are heavier than the ones you will use in the arena," he explains. "Your real gear will seem much lighter and easier to use."

Telephus leads you to a pole in the courtyard. You begin to thrust your sword and then move back and forth and around the pole. "Yes, you must move," Telephus says. "But not too much. You don't want to tire yourself."

A murmillo (left) fought a retiarius (right) in Pompeii's amphitheatre.

The training is hard, but you become more confident each day. The time comes for you to train with a sica. Telephus watches carefully as you spar with another gladiator. "You've learned well," he says.

The day of your first match arrives. Your opponent is a murmillo named Severus. Like all murmillones, he carries a large, rectangular shield and a gladius. Severus has fought many matches and has won most of them.

As the match begins, you move forward and fake a stab to Severus' right. He moves his shield against the blow. You lunge and stab his left hip. The crowd roars as Severus goes down. They are amazed you have drawn blood with your first thrust. You move in closer. But as you concentrate on his sword, he uses his shield to trip you. Now you're both on the ground.

*Turn the page.*

You jump up quickly, but Severus remains on the ground. You catch Severus with a jab just above his right leg armour. His blood flows into the sand.

"You can ask for mercy," you say. "The crowd will spare a great fighter like you."

"Never," Severus says.

✚To keep fighting, turn to page **65**.
✚To walk away, turn to page **67**.

You stand there silently, staring across the courtyard.

"Hey, *novicius*," Cresces says, giving you a shove. "Time to start your training."

"I need to go to the toilet," you say.

You hand the weapons to him. He points you in the right direction, towards the school's kitchen. As you walk, you look behind you. The trainers and gladiators are busy. Cresces is nowhere in sight.

You see a passageway leading out of the school. You bolt through the passageway and onto the street. You stop running and begin to walk. No one but your family knows you went to the school. Anyone who sees you will think you are still a free citizen.

*Turn the page.*

You walk through the town. You can't go home, or Pomponius will find you and punish you. You head into the countryside. You don't know where to go next. Perhaps Naples, just 24 kilometres (15 miles) away. Maybe even Rome itself. And you will forget you ever dreamed of being a gladiator.

## THE END

*To follow another path, turn to page 11.*
*To read the conclusion, turn to page 101.*

"I can't fight Florus," you tell Pomponius. "He is too experienced. I think I should fight another novicius."

"You refuse to follow your master's orders?" Pomponius yells. In a flash, he swings his hand across your face. "Just for that, I should send you against the best secutor I have. Let him kill you before you even get a chance to throw your net." Pomponius shoves you against the wall. "But then I would have wasted all the money I spent training you."

Pomponius leads you to a cell. Inside, he locks you to chains bolted into the wall. Two other prisoners are already chained.

"A few weeks in here will help you remember that you are a slave now," Pomponius says. "Next time you will fight whoever I tell you to."

*Turn the page.*

You slump to the floor. You hear the footsteps of the other gladiators walking to the amphitheatre. And you wonder why you ever wanted to become a gladiator.

Disobedient gladiators were punished by being chained in tiny rooms.

✝

## THE END

*To follow another path, turn to page 11.*
*To read the conclusion, turn to page 101.*

"Come on," Cresces says. "You knew someday you'd have to fight Florus."

You know he's right. But you never expected it to happen so soon. Still, you will honour your oath. You will fight Florus.

You and the other gladiators parade out of the school and head towards the amphitheatre. About 20,000 fans wait for you, eager to see skilled combat. You and Florus will fight the first match.

You stand barefoot on the sand. In your left hand, you hold your net, while your right clutches your trident. You stare at Florus, barely seeing his eyes through the visor on his helmet. He clutches his gladius in one hand and his shield in the other.

*Turn the page.*

A retiarius fought with a net and a three-pronged weapon called a trident.

An umpire stands to the side, holding a wooden stick. He is ready to force you back into the fight if you try to flee. But as a retiarius, you are allowed to run a bit, in order to prepare yourself to attack again.

Before you can move, Florus charges at you, his shield held high. You try to move away, but trip on your own net. You scramble to get up. Florus stands above you. His sword nicks your shoulder. Pain sears through your right arm, and you drop your trident.

As Florus prepares to strike again, you stagger to your feet. You hurl your net, but it misses Florus. You turn to run, but he smacks you with his shield. Lying on the ground, you hold up your right index finger. This gesture signals that you are begging for mercy.

*Turn the page.*

Boos and shouts fill the arena. The editor will decide whether you will live or die. He decides to let you live. A doctor rushes over to look at your wound. You didn't fight well, but you managed to survive your first fight. Next time you'll do better.

## THE END

*To follow another path, turn to page 11.*
*To read the conclusion, turn to page 101.*

"I'm ready," you say. Telephus calls for another trainer to bring over armour and a sword for you. "Normally you would never fight another thraex," Telephus says, "but today I'll make an exception."

You struggle to strap on the leg armour and the *manica* that covers your right arm. You put on the bronze helmet. The visor has small metal plates with holes in them. Even with the holes, it's not easy to see.

"Here," Telephus says. "Take your sword." The sica feels different from your grandfather's old gladius. Everything feels different. And wrong.

You keep your eye on Telephus' sword, ready to move your shield to ward off a thrust. He moves forward with the blade, and you block it with your shield.

*Turn the page.*

But you don't see his shield swinging at you from the side. Like a club, it crashes into your helmet. You stagger backwards, then fall. In an instant, Telephus is standing over you. His sword is raised above your head.

"Do you want some more?" he asks. Some of the other gladiators call, *"Habet, hoc habet"* – the Roman cry for "He's got it!" It means a gladiator is about to die.

"N-no, Telephus," you say. "No more."

"Good. Now maybe you can begin your training. And learn to obey me."

"Yes, sir," you reply. You've just learned your first lesson as a gladiator.

✠

## THE END

*To follow another path, turn to page 11.*
*To read the conclusion, turn to page 101.*

64

The crowd shouts as they see Severus in pain. He struggles to one knee. With his last strength, he lunges at you with his sword. You easily step away. You take your shield and swing it against his head.

Severus is too weak to defend himself from the blow. He falls on his back, and you stand above him. You look over at the editor. He will decide whether Severus lives or dies.

Some of the fans call for Severus' death. But most remember his past fights, his bravery and skill. They call, "*Mitte*," which means, "Let him go." The editor agrees and signals his decision to the umpire.

Men bring out a stretcher to carry Severus to the doctor. If his wounds aren't serious, he'll fight again.

*Turn the page.*

You walk over to where the editor sits. He hands you an olive branch and money for winning the match.

"An impressive victory," he says. "We look forward to seeing more of you in the arena."

You bow slightly and thank him. Then you smile, knowing your career as a gladiator has started very well.

## THE END

*To follow another path, turn to page 11.*
*To read the conclusion, turn to page 101.*

You don't want to hurt Severus anymore. You begin to cross the chalk lines drawn in the sand, which mark where the fighting takes place. The umpire walks towards you.

"Stop." He holds his stick in front of you. "You haven't won yet."

"He's hurt," you say. "He can't defeat me."

"Keep fighting," the umpire replies. "Remember your oath."

You turn back towards Severus. He's pulled himself to his feet, but he leans on his shield for support.

"I'm not afraid to die," he says to you. "But maybe you're afraid to kill me."

*Turn the page.*

Anger burns inside you. You are afraid of nothing. With your sword, you pull Severus' shield away. He tumbles to the ground. Even on his back, he swings wildly with his gladius. You take one more stab at his chest with your sica. As you pull out the blade, you know he is dead.

Some people in the crowd don't like your style. They wanted to help decide Severus' fate. But most see Severus would never have given up. And you have fought well. With this first victory, you are the new hero of the games.

You go back to the school. In the following days, you sometimes feel the earth shake. One day in August, you hear a rumbling from Mount Vesuvius. The volcano begins to shoot out ash, deadly gases, and volcanic rocks.

Mount Vesuvius erupted on 24 August 79, destroying the city of Pompeii.

You stand in the street in horror. You turn to run, but have taken only a few steps when the ash comes raining down. You take your last breath as it buries you where you fall.

### THE END

*To follow another path, turn to page 11.*
*To read the conclusion, turn to page 101.*

The murmillo fought
with a short sword
called a gladius.

# CHAPTER 4

# A champion's last fight

You sit at a long table covered with food including fish, chicken, and all sorts of wild game. The editor of tomorrow's games has spared no expense for this feast. It's not surprising, since the editor is none other than Emperor Trajan himself.

Tomorrow is special for another reason. If you win, it will be your last fight. The lanista, who owns you, has promised that Trajan will award you the *rudis*. This wooden sword rewards your skill over many years of combat. Most of all, it signals that you are a free man. You will no longer be a slave. No longer a gladiator.

*Turn the page.*

A senator is sitting nearby with another wealthy man. "My cousin here has never seen you fight," he says. "Tell him about yourself."

"I am a slave, and many years ago I was a criminal," you reply. "My punishment was to become a gladiator. I have fought as a murmillo for more than 15 years."

"Ah, yes, the murmillo, with your gladius, grand helmet, and large shield. You have fought dozens of times. You have almost always won. You are popular across Italy."

You nod.

"And you have killed many men," the senator adds. You nod again. So many of the Romans enjoy the death they see in the arena. For you, it is just part of your job.

After the feast you return to the school where you live and train. You have a wife and children, but they live in a house in the city. Late the next morning, you prepare for the parade from the barracks to the great Flavian Amphitheatre.

As you march, musicians play. Inside, the crowd has already watched the animal hunts. For these games, Trajan has brought in thousands of wild animals from across the empire. Bears and bulls, lions and leopards, and even giraffes and crocodiles. Hunters called *venatores* kill the less dangerous animals. Other men, called *bestiarii*, fight the deadlier beasts, such as lions.

As you reach the amphitheatre, the lanista approaches you. "You can choose the type of opponent for today, either a thraex or a hoplomachus. But I'll still choose the gladiator, to make sure the fight is fair."

*Turn the page.*

A bestiarius fought lions and other fierce animals.

You often fight a thraex, with his curved

sword. A hoplomachus has a much shorter

dagger and a small shield, but he uses a spear as

well. Either can be a difficult opponent.

✝To *fight a hoplomachus, go to page* **75**.

✝To *fight a thraex, turn to page* **81**.

It will be good to fight a hoplomachus.

As you're about to enter the amphitheatre, you see a man talking to the lanista. He's the senator you spoke to at the feast.

"Come here," the lanista calls to you. You step out of line as the other gladiators enter the building.

"I travel often to the far reaches of the empire," the senator tells you. "I want you to serve as my bodyguard."

"Perhaps you can hire me after I win today," you say. "I'll be a free man, and we can discuss a salary."

"But what if you don't win?" the senator says.

*Turn the page.*

"Then maybe I wasn't the best man to be your bodyguard. Besides, it's not up to me," you say. You point to the lanista. "I'm still his slave."

"The senator has made a generous offer," the lanista says. "But you may decide for yourself. You can go with the senator or fight for the rudis you deserve."

✢To enter the arena and fight, go to page 77.
✢To become the senator's bodyguard, turn to page 85.

"Thank you," you tell the senator. "But I want to win my freedom or die trying." You continue into the amphitheatre.

You and the other gladiators begin your warm-ups. You use wooden weapons. You spar with another gladiator to stretch your muscles and prepare for the fight.

Blacksmiths take out the real swords and feel their blades to make sure they are sharp. The crowd wants to see that the swords will do their job.

You wait in a lower part of the arena for your turn to fight. As you and your opponent enter the arena, the crowd stands and roars its approval. Fans shout your name.

*Turn the page.*

The hoplomachus holds his spear in his right hand. He thrusts it at you, trying to slip its sharp point beyond your shield. But your shield blocks each thrust. You hack at the spear with your sword. You must break the spear or make him drop it, so you can move in closer.

You and your opponent circle each other. After a spear thrust, you swing your shield up at the long weapon. The hoplomachus loses his grip. You strike your sword on the spear's shaft, causing your opponent to drop it. Before he can pick it up again, you rush forward. Now you have him!

The hoplomachus swings his dagger, but your sword keeps him a safe distance away. You move closer. Several of your thrusts get past his shield, but his body is covered with padding and armour.

A hoplomachus was named after a heavily armed Greek soldier called a hoplite. They wore similar gear.

*Turn the page.*

You give a sharp thrust that pierces through your opponent's padding. The hoplomachus falls to the ground.

The audience calls, "Finish him off! Let him have it!"

You could go in for the kill. But this is your last fight. Maybe you should let the crowd see more of your skills.

✝To close in on your opponent, turn to page **87**.
✝To pull back, turn to page **89**.

The thraex is a good match for you. You're almost equal in the armour you wear, although your shield is bigger.

You straighten your helmet as you walk into the amphitheatre. The thraex is already inside, waiting for you. You can't see his face through the small metal holes on the front of his helmet. Just as well, since it's easier to kill a man if you don't know who he is.

Even before the fight begins, you have a decision to make. You can take the offensive by attacking him quickly and overpowering him with your strength. Or you can go on the defensive and hope to tire him out.

✝To go on the defensive, turn to page **82**.
✝To go on the offensive, turn to page **92**.

You circle around the thraex, waiting for him to attack. He thrusts several times with his curved sword, but you block each blow. You make a few weak thrusts of your own. You want him to think you are slow and too old to fight well.

For several minutes the arena echoes with the sound of your opponent's sword battering your shield. Now his strikes are slower. He is beginning to tire.

You move closer, moving your sword with more power. Then your sword catches his shoulder. The crowd roars with delight.

You raise your sword, urging the crowd to cheer louder. Then with a burst of speed, the thraex comes at you. He slips the edge of his shield under yours, raising it. With your side exposed, he quickly jabs his sword into your ribs.

You've been foolish! You know not to let your guard down. You bend over in pain, barely able to raise your sword.

The thraex comes at you again, but this time you block the blow. You are both bloody and staggering. With your head down, you hold up your right index finger, the signal that you have had enough. As you look to see how the emperor will react, you see your opponent has done the same thing.

The crowd shouts, *"Missio!"*

The fans want both of you to be released. The emperor agrees. He calls both of you over. The lanista's slaves help you walk to the emperor's seat. The slaves then call for a stretcher and a doctor.

*Turn the page.*

"You have earned the wooden sword your lanista promised you," the emperor tells you.

"So, what will you do now?" a senator nearby asks. "Will you fight as a free man? Will you leave the arena forever?"

Before the match you thought you knew what you would do if you won the rudis. Now you aren't so sure.

✢To continue fighting as a free man,
turn to page 96.

✢To stop fighting, turn to page 98.

You're not sure you can beat the hoplomachus. And a wound from your last match never completely healed. Working for the senator would be a much easier life.

"Will I still be a slave if I go with you?" you ask the senator.

"Yes, but not for long. I will free you after one year, as long as you continue to work for me."

You hear the roar of the crowd from inside the amphitheatre. You know so well the thrill of fighting in front of the emperor. But the senator's offer is a good one.

"I'll go with you," you say.

"Excellent!" the senator says. "My servant will take you to my home."

*Turn the page.*

The Flavian Amphitheatre held about 50,000 people.

The Flavian Amphitheatre held about 50,000 people.

The senator and the lanista enter the amphitheatre. You turn away and follow your new master's servant. Your days as a gladiator are over.

## THE END

*To follow another path, turn to page 11.*
*To read the conclusion, turn to page 101.*

You move in carefully. Your opponent still has his dagger. But he looks beaten. He struggles to get up. With one blow of your sword to the side of his helmet, you knock him onto the sand. You step on his hand, and he releases his weapon. Everyone in the arena knows he is finished.

You look towards the emperor. He has the power to release the fallen gladiator. Or, with Trajan's word, you will deliver the coup de grace – the final blow that kills your opponent. But Trajan will not decide alone. He wants to keep the support of the common people. Letting them decide what happens is one way to do this.

The people shout and motion with their thumbs. Some call for your opponent's death, while others want to spare him. But since you are so popular, and your opponent isn't, the decision is easy. He will die.

*Turn the page.*

Each fighter knows how he must face death. The hoplomachus struggles to one knee. He grabs your upper leg. You hold his helmet, now warmed by the strong afternoon sun. You move his head so his neck is exposed. You thrust your sword through it, killing him instantly.

The crowd roars again as you walk to the emperor's box. An official comes down to the arena to hand you the wooden sword. You now have your freedom. Your days as a gladiator are over.

✠

## THE END

*To follow another path, turn to page 11.*
*To read the conclusion, turn to page 101.*

Maybe a break is good for you too. You realize how much your muscles ache. Even though the hoplomachus never landed a clean hit, he has worn you down. You circle him as he draws himself up to one knee.

The hoplomachus stands, bleeding and breathing heavily. But he's not ready to quit. With a sudden burst of energy, he goes to your right. You realize too late that he's scrambling for his spear. You turn but can't beat him to it. Now the crowd senses the match might be even again.

The two of you again face each other in the centre of the arena. But you're both exhausted now. The umpire steps between you.

"Water!" he cries. Two slaves run out carrying water for each of you. You open the visor of your helmet and guzzle the cool water. The break is short, but you feel a bit stronger now.

*Turn the page.*

But your opponent has regained some strength too. His wound is not as bad as you thought. And he has his spear again. Your shield feels heavy in your left hand. You move it to stop his spear, but one thrust slices into your thigh. You hold back a shout of pain as you fall to the sand.

The hoplomachus stabs again. You feel weaker than you ever have. You finally get up to one knee, but your opponent is upon you, his dagger out. You stop, knowing he can kill you.

You hold up your right index finger, to show you have accepted defeat. The emperor will decide whether you live or die. But he will listen to the crowd.

Gladiators begged for the editor's mercy by raising an index finger.

Shouts of *"Mitte"* – "Release him!" – fill the amphitheatre. The Romans want you to live, and Trajan agrees. But you will have to fight another day to earn your freedom.

## THE END

*To follow another path, turn to page 11.*
*To read the conclusion, turn to page 101.*

You quickly move forward, hoping to catch the thraex off guard. You thrust your sword to the right, left, up, and down to see how he reacts. He is quicker defending himself when you move to his right, his sword side. So you will focus on the left.

You circle the thraex, holding up your huge shield. He thrusts a few times with his sword, but your shield easily blocks it.

Your opponent is younger than you. He moves easily on his feet. You had hoped to tire him out with your burst of energy at the beginning. But now you're the one feeling tired. You slow down a bit, and some people in the crowd don't like it.

"Come on!" you hear someone shout. "Fight him! Are you afraid?"

Afraid? What do these people know about fear, about facing death? You'll show them.

"Ahh!" you yell, charging forward. You thrust, and the thraex raises his shield to block it. His sword comes at you, but you step aside. You use your shield like a club and swing as he steps past you. The blow sends him staggering, but he regains his balance. The crowd roars its approval.

Once again you go forward. You thrust high, but the thraex is ready for the blow. He ducks down, goes to one knee, and reaches his shield arm towards you. Before you can step away, you feel a hand pulling on your leg. You tumble to the ground as your shield flies out of your hand.

As you lie on your back, the thraex quickly scrambles over you. As his sword comes down, you roll away just in time.

*Turn the page.*

The thraex grunts as the sword digs into the sand. You start to get up and grab for your shield, but the thraex jabs at your uncovered left arm. The blade cuts into your flesh. Bleeding, you manage to get to one knee. The crowd has quieted a bit. They think you might lose.

The thraex stands between you and your shield. All you have is your sword. You thrust carefully, knowing your left side is exposed. He blocks the thrust. Then with a lightning-fast motion, he stabs his sword into your chest.

You fall to the ground, and your eyes start to close. You were too old and slow, and your opponent was too skilled. But at least you know you died an honourable death and will have a good burial. You have saved your winnings over the years. Your wife will take care of everything. Then you will enter the underworld ruled by the god Pluto, where all spirits of the dead go.

Gladiators' wives feared that their husbands would be killed in the arena.

✠

## THE END

*To follow another path, turn to page 11.*
*To read the conclusion, turn to page 101.*

"Fighting is all I know," you say. "And I think I do it pretty well."

The officials around the emperor laugh. They know you are one of the best gladiators Rome has ever seen.

"You can fight for me as a free man," the lanista says. "I know you can make plenty of money across the empire."

"The money would be good," you say. "I have my family to support."

"Good," the emperor says. "I will enjoy watching you fight again."

You leave the emperor and are helped to the stretcher. The doctor will treat your wound in the lower area of the amphitheatre.

Doctors tended to injured gladiators who survived their matches.

As you wait, slaves across the amphitheatre begin to throw small wooden balls into the crowd. Each ball has the name of a gift on it, such as a horse or a silver vase. Anyone who catches a ball can claim the gift written on it. But you don't need gifts. You have your freedom.

## THE END

*To follow another path, turn to page 11.*
*To read the conclusion, turn to page 101.*

"I've had enough," you say. "I know some gladiators fight till they are older than I am. But I want to find a job and raise my family."

"What will you do?" the senator asks.

"He can work for me," the lanista says. "I could use a skilled murmillo like you to train the young fighters."

"I accept," you say. As a trainer, you can still use your skills without risking your life. And you can stay near the barracks that you know so well.

"Good," the lanista says. "When can you start work at the school?"

"Let's see what the doctor says about my wound," you say as you lie on the waiting stretcher. "Then give me a few days with my family. After that, I'll be ready to work."

"To train the next great gladiator, perhaps?" the senator says.

You smile. "There will never be another gladiator like me."

## THE END

*To follow another path, turn to page 11.*
*To read the conclusion, turn to page 101.*

The monk Telemachus (centre) was killed trying to stop a gladiator match in 404.

# CHAPTER 5

# The last years of the gladiators

For many years the gladiatorial games were part of what some Romans called "bread and circuses". The emperors provided the citizens free wheat for bread and public games to entertain them. With the bread and games, the people were happy and less likely to rebel.

Gladiatorial games were like today's films and sporting events. They were sources of entertainment that helped people forget their daily troubles. People even bought art and items such as vases and lamps decorated with images of gladiators.

The ruins of the Colosseum still stand in Rome today.

The emperors kept tight control over the games. They wanted to prevent slave rebellions, like the one at the school where Spartacus trained.

The Flavian Amphitheatre in Rome was the centre of the most spectacular games. This huge amphitheatre was later called the Colosseum. Other cities in Italy and in other parts of the empire also hosted games.

But by the AD 200s, Rome's emperors sometimes struggled to find money to run the empire. The games remained popular, but in many parts of the empire, they were not as large as they had been in the past. Some Romans opposed the games because of their cruelty, but the opponents had little influence with the emperors.

Christian leaders were also against the violent games. For years Roman emperors opposed Christianity, because the religion said the Romans should give up their gods and worship only the Christian god. But in 312 Emperor Constantine declared himself a Christian. The Christian faith then became more popular throughout the empire.

Constantine technically outlawed the gladiatorial games in 325. But gladiatorial combats continued into the early 400s. After that, written records still described the animal hunts and mass executions of the past. But the gladiators were not mentioned.

By this time the Roman Empire had split into eastern and western halves. The western empire fell in 476. Roman laws and culture continued in the eastern half, known as Byzantium. The hunts continued there for a time.

Europeans later invented new contests for two fighters. During the Middle Ages, knights on horseback charged at each other with long spears called lances. These jousts could be deadly. Bullfighting, which developed in Spain, pitted a man against a bull in the arena. Some people have compared bullfighters to the ancient gladiators.

Today boxers and mixed martial artists fight in front of cheering crowds. Their bodies replace the gladiators' weapons and shields, and no one fights to the death. But modern audiences cheer as the Romans did, admiring the fighters' bravery and skill.

The gladiators' fights started as small ceremonies to honour the dead. They grew into grand social events that honoured the glory of a great empire. The gladiators also displayed the bravery in battle that the Romans admired and the bravery they hoped to show when they faced their own death some day.

# TIME LINE

**753 BC** – The city of Rome is founded, according to
   Roman legend.

**Middle 300s BC** – People of Campania, a region outside
   Rome, paint gladiators in combat on grave walls.

**264 BC** – First recorded gladiatorial games take place
   in Rome.

**186 BC** – Animals are first included as part of the games.

**73 BC** – Spartacus leads a rebellion of gladiators
   and slaves.

**71 BC** – The Romans end Spartacus' rebellion.

**27 BC** – Augustus becomes the first Roman emperor.

**AD 59** – Fans riot at the amphitheatre in Pompeii.
   The emperor shuts down gladiatorial games there
   for 10 years.

**63** – Emperor Nero holds games that feature wealthy
   Romans, both men and women, as gladiators.

**79** – The eruption of Mount Vesuvius destroys the city
   of Pompeii.

**80** – The Flavian Amphitheatre, later called the
   Colosseum, opens in Rome.

**81 – 96**–Emperor Domitian, who built four major gladiator schools near the Colosseum, rules the Roman Empire.

**107** – Emperor Trajan holds games to celebrate his victory in Dacia.

**117** – The Roman Empire reaches its peak size.

**180s** – Emperor Commodus often fights as a gladiator, using the name "Hercules the Hunter."

**200** – Emperor Septimius Severus bans women from competing as gladiators.

**325** – Emperor Constantine outlaws gladiatorial games, although many still take place during the next 100 years.

**395** – The Roman Empire splits into eastern and western halves, each with its own emperor.

**404** – Games are stopped for a time in Rome after a crowd kills the Christian monk Telemachus, who was trying to stop a fight between gladiators.

**476** – The Roman Empire collapses in western Europe. The eastern empire continues and is known as the Byzantine Empire.

# OTHER PATHS TO EXPLORE

In this book you've seen how stories of gladiators look different from three points of view.

Perspectives on history are as varied as the people who lived it. You can explore other paths on your own to learn more about what happened. Seeing history from many points of view is an important part of understanding it.

Here are some ideas for other gladiator points of view to explore:

- ◆ Venatores and bestiarii were not gladiators, but they competed at gladiator events by hunting and fighting animals. What were their lives like?

- ◆ A few women served as gladiators. How were their experiences different from those of male gladiators?

- ◆ Many Romans enjoyed the bloody gladiator battles. What would it be like to be a spectator at the games?

# READ MORE

*All About Life in Ancient Rome*, Brenda and Brian Williams, (Raintree, 2014)

*Gladiators and Roman Soldiers*, Charlotte Guillain (Raintree, 2010)

*Gladiator: The Roman Fighter's (Unofficial) Manual*, Philip Matyszak (Thames and Hudson, 2011)

*Greatest Warriors: Gladiators*, Alex Stewart (Franklin Watts, 2014 )

# INTERNET SITES

Visit these websites to find out more about Roman gladiators:

www.bbc.co.uk/schools/primaryhistory/romans/leisure/

www.history.com/news/history-lists/10-things-you-may-not-know-about-roman-gladiators

www.salariya.com/web_books/gladiator/index.html

# GLOSSARY

**amphitheatre** – large, open-air building with rows of seats around an arena

**auctoratus** – free Roman citizen who volunteered to become a gladiator

**Celtic** – relating to the Celts, a people who lived in parts of western and central Europe

**hoplomachus** – gladiator who fought with a dagger, spear, and small shield

**murmillo** – gladiator who fought with a sword and a large shield

**novicius** – person training to become a gladiator

**retiarius** – gladiator who fought with a net and trident

**rudis** – wooden sword given to a gladiator, meaning he has won his freedom

**secutor** – gladiator with a sword and shield who usually fought a retiarius

**thraex** – gladiator who fought with a curved sword

# BIBLIOGRAPHY

**Adkins, Lesley, and Roy A. Adkins.** *Handbook to Life in Ancient Rome.* New York: Oxford University Press, 1998.

**Carcopino, Jerome.** *Daily Life in Ancient Rome.* New Haven, Conn.: Yale University Press, 2003.

**Crowther, Nigel B.** *Sport in Ancient Times.* Westport, Conn.: Praeger Publishers, 2007.

**Jacobelli, Luciana.** *Gladiators at Pompeii.* Rome: L'Erma di Bretschneider, 2003.

**Meijer, Fik.** *The Gladiators.* New York: Thomas Dunne Books, 2004.

**Shadrake, Susanna.** *The World of the Gladiator.* Stroud, U.K: Tempus, 2005.

**Shelton, Jo-Ann.** *As the Romans Did: A Sourcebook in Roman Social History.* New York: Oxford University Press, 1998.

**Strauss, Barry.** *The Spartacus War.* New York: Simon and Schuster, 2009.

**Wiedemann, Thomas E. J.** *Emperors and Gladiators.* London: Routledge, 1992.

**Winkler, Martin M., ed.** *Spartacus: Film and History.* Malden, Mass.: Blackwell Publishing, 2007.

# INDEX